TREASURE ISLAND

THE KINGSWOOD
PLAYS FOR BOYS AND GIRLS

THE KING WHO TOOK SUNSHINE	James Reeves
MULCASTER MARKET	James Reeves
TREASURE ISLAND	Malcolm Morgan
SIX PLAYS FOR GIRLS	N. L. Clay
THE PLAY OF THE ROYAL ASTROLOGERS	Willis Hall
THE SERVANTS OF TWO MASTERS	Carlo Goldoni
THE LIAR	Carlo Goldoni
THE TIME EXPLORERS	Marie Overton

TREASURE ISLAND

*

AN ADVENTURE IN THREE ACTS
ADAPTED FROM
R. L. STEVENSON'S NOVEL

*

by

MALCOLM MORGAN

HEINEMANN
EDUCATIONAL

Heinemann Educational Publishers
Halley Court, Jordan Hill, Oxford OX2 8EJ
A Division of Reed Educational & Professional Publishing Ltd

OXFORD MELBOURNE AUCKLAND
JOHANNESBURG BLANTYRE GABORONE
IBADAN PORTSMOUTH (NH) USA CHICAGO

ISBN 0 435 21001 7

© COPYRIGHT 1954 – MALCOLM MORGAN

FIRST PUBLISHED 1954

00 01 27

*All rights whatsoever in this play are strictly reserved
and applications for productions, etc., should be made to:
International Copyright Bureau Ltd,
Suite 8, 26 Charing Cross Road,
London WC2H 0DG*

Printed and bound in Great Britain by
Athenaeum Press Ltd, Gateshead, Tyne & Wear.

"If this don't fetch 'em, kids have gone rotten since my day."

R. L. Stevenson, 1881.

CHARACTERS

Captain Billy Bones
Jim Hawkins
Dr. Livesey
Mrs. Hawkins
Black Dog
Blind Pew
Tom Morgan
Squire Trelawney
Long John Silver
Mrs. Trefuddle
Mrs. McGoo
Dead-Bones Jones
Captain Smollett
Ben Gunn

Act One

Scene 1. The Admiral Benbow Inn, Blackhill Cove, N. Devon. A late afternoon in Spring 1783.

Scene 2. The same. Morning, two days later.

Scene 3. The same. Afternoon, two weeks later.

Act Two

Scene 1. The *Hispaniola* at sea, several weeks later.

Scene 2. Treasure Island, next morning.

Act Three

Scene 1. Treasure Island, one second later.

Scene 2. Treasure Island, the next day.

TREASURE ISLAND

ACT I

Scene 1

At the Admiral Benbow Inn, Blackhill Cove, N. Devon.

There is a door up right leading to the Captain's room, a door up left leading to the porch and other parts of the house, and a door down left to the kitchen. There is a bench and table with two chairs below the door up right and another in front of the window, centre, and yet another down stage, left.

It is a late afternoon in spring, 1783.

THE CAPTAIN, *an old seadog of about sixty, with a vivid scar on his right cheek, is discovered at the table right, drinking. He is very drunk.*

CAPTAIN: Jim, more rum. More rum, I say, Jim.

JIM (*off*): Coming, Captain. Coming.

Enter JIM.

CAPTAIN: More rum, Jim. More rum.

JIM: Yes, Captain. (JIM *turns to go.*)

Enter DR. LIVESEY.

DR. LIVESEY (*good-naturedly*): What's all this noise about?

CAPTAIN (*shouts*): Silence there between decks.

DR. LIVESEY: Were you addressing me, sir?

CAPTAIN (*rising*): Ar! Silence I say.

DR. LIVESEY: I have only one thing to say to you, sir, and that is that if you keep on drinking rum the world will soon be quit of a very dirty scoundrel.

CAPTAIN (*draws knife and threatens* DOCTOR): Scoundrel, you say?

DR. LIVESEY: Put that knife away or upon my honour you shall hang at the next Assizes.

THE CAPTAIN *does so.*

DR. LIVESEY: And now, sir, since I know there is such a fellow in my district, you may count I will have an eye open night and day. I am not only a doctor, I am also a magistrate, and if I catch a breath of complaint against you, if it is only for a piece of incivility like this, I will take effectual means to have you hunted down and routed out. And as a doctor I will tell you this—one glass of rum won't kill you, but if you take one you'll take another and then another, and I stake my wig if you don't break off short you'll die. Do you understand that?—die. Now, come on, Jim, we will help him to bed.

Exeunt everyone; BLACK DOG *appears at the window.* JIM *and the* DOCTOR *return;* BLACK DOG *disappears.*

DR. LIVESEY: How long has that old seadog been here, Jim?

JIM: About six months, Doctor. One day he just came and said, 'This is a handy cove and a pleasantly situated grog-shop. Is there much company, mate?' I told him there wasn't. Then he said, 'This is the place for me.'

Enter MRS. HAWKINS.

MRS. HAWKINS: And what about the money, Jim? Tell

the doctor about the money. Threw down three pieces of gold, he did, and said, 'You can tell me when I have worked through that.' Well, he has worked through it, twice over, and I have told him and I've still not got any more.

DR. LIVESEY (*laughs*): Well, be sure he does not drink any more rum, Mrs. Hawkins, and keep your eye on young Jim, or he'll be running away to sea. (*Exit.*)

MRS. HAWKINS: Hurry up with them pots, Jim. We might have some company tonight. Lord knows it's hard enough not having your poor father with us, without you sitting and listening to that old ruffian's sea stories.

JIM: But, Mother . . .

MRS. HAWKINS: If you ask me he was probably a pirate. That old sea chest of his looks like a pirate's chest. (*Exit.*)

JIM *laughs and sings*.

JIM: Fifteen men on the dead man's chest—
Yo-ho-ho, and a bottle of rum!
Drink and the devil had done for the rest—
Yo-ho-ho, and a bottle of rum.

He picks up empty bottle from table, right, on 'rum', turns to go left, as BLACK DOG *enters.* JIM *starts and drops the bottle. It has been getting darker throughout the scene.*

BLACK DOG: Come here, Sonny, come nearer here. Now, Sonny, is my mate, Bill, about?

JIM (*very nervous*): No, sir, there is only my mother—and me . . . and the Captain.

BLACK DOG: Well, my mate Bill will be called the Captain as like as not. A cut on one cheek he has, and a mighty pleasant way with him, particularly in drink, has my mate, Bill. We'll put it for argument like that your

Captain has a cut on one cheek and we'll put it if you like that that cheek is the right one.

During this he has moved slowly across to JIM, *grasped him by his left arm, turned him so that he is facing down stage right and moved him slowly towards the door, right.*

Now, is my mate Bill in this house?

JIM: N-n-no, sir, he is out.
Noise off. THE CAPTAIN'S *voice heard singing 'Yo-ho-ho', etc.* BLACK DOG *pushes* JIM *away left.*

BLACK DOG: Little boys shouldn't lie. Tain't h-onest.

BLACK DOG *hides behind door.* THE CAPTAIN *enters and goes centre.*

Bill! (CAPTAIN *starts.*) Come, Bill, you know me. You know an old shipmate, surely.

CAPTAIN: Black Dog!!

BLACK DOG: And who else? (*Seeing* JIM *still there.*) Be off with you and none of your keyholes, sonny.
Exit JIM.

CAPTAIN: Well, you've run me down. Here I am. What is it?

BLACK DOG: We want it, Billy. You've got it and we want it, and we mean to have it.

CAPTAIN: Got what?

BLACK DOG: You know what. Flint's fist, that's what. Flint's fist, as belongs to all his crew and not just one.

CAPTAIN: Well, you can go back and tell 'em, Morgan, Pew, Silver, all of 'em, that I'll see them in hell before I part with what's mine.

He draws his cutlass. They exchange a few blows and BLACK DOG *flees.* THE CAPTAIN *staggers back to the table hand at heart, and sits.*

CAPTAIN: Jim, Jim. (*Enter* JIM.) Bring me a noggin of rum, Jim.

JIM: Remember what the doctor said, Captain.

CAPTAIN: The devil take the doctor. Doctors is all swabs, and that doctor there, why, what do he know about seafaring men? I been in places hot as pitch with men dropping all around me with yellow jack and fever, the blessed land heaving like the sea with earthquakes. What do the doctor know of lands like that? And I lived on rum, I tell you. It's been meat and drink, man and wife to me. Look, Jim, how my fingers fidget. I can't keep them still. I've had no more than a thimbleful this day. If I don't have some rum, Jim, I'll have the horrors. I've seen some of them already. I've seen old Flint in the corner there behind you—as plain as print I seen him—and if I get the horrors, I'm a man that has lived rough and I'll raise Cain. The doctor said one glass wouldn't hurt me. I'll give you a golden guinea for a noggin.

JIM: I want none of your money, but what you owe my mother. I'll get you one glass and no more.

JIM *gets the rum, while he is out* THE CAPTAIN *makes sure a key is still on a string round his neck. Enter* JIM.

CAPTAIN: Did you hear something, Jim?

JIM: No.

CAPTAIN: Quick, to the window, Jim. Are there any seafaring men about? A blind man, perhaps? Or a man with one leg? Keep a sharp eye out for a man with one leg, Jim.

JIM: Yes, Captain. I will. A man with one leg.

CAPTAIN: If he's about I'm done for. That was Black Dog that was just here, Jim. He's a bad 'un. But there's worse that put him on. And if I can't get away, they'll tip me the Black Spot. Listen, Jim; it's my sea chest they're after, but they mustn't get it. I'd rather be hanged and have them hang with me. You stay here and send your mother down to that doctor swab. Tell him to pipe all hands—magistrates, revenue men and such, and lay 'em aboard the Admiral Benbow, because there he'll find all Flint's crew—all of 'em that's left. Hurry, lad, hurry.

JIM: Y-yes, Captain. (JIM *exits quickly.*)

CAPTAIN: They'll not get me. I'll beat them yet. Old Billy Bones'll beat them yet. Rum! More rum!

He drinks. JIM *returns.*

JIM: Mother's gone. You shouldn't be drinking all that rum.

CAPTAIN: I was his mate, I was. Old Flint's first mate, and I'm the only one that knows the place. He gave it to me in Savannah when he lay a-dying. But you won't tell about that, will you, Jim? Unless they get the Black Spot on me or you see that sea-faring man with one leg, Jim, him above all.

JIM: But what is the Black Spot, Captain?

CAPTAIN: It's a summons, mate, like the angel of death.

BLIND PEW's *stick is heard—tap, tap, tap.*

BLIND PEW (*off*): Will any kind friend inform a poor blind man, who's lost the precious sight of his eyes in the gracious defence of his native country—God bless King George—in what part of the country he is?

JIM (*going to door*): At the Admiral Benbow, sir, Blackhill Co . . .

JIM starts back with a cry of horror as BLIND PEW *enters. He is a tall, gaunt man, dressed in a black robe and hood, so that only his hands and face show. A black bandage is tied round his eyes. He is very pale.*

BLIND PEW: I heard a voice—a young voice. Will you give me your hand, kind friend, and lead me in?

JIM does not move. BLIND PEW *taps slowly towards him, goes past him and suddenly lunges out and seizes him, twisting his arm behind his back.*

Now, boy, take me to the Captain or I'll break your arm.

THE CAPTAIN *drops his glass.* BLIND PEW *thrusts* JIM *aside.*

Now, Bill, stay where you are. If I can't see, I can hear a finger stirring. Business is business. Hold out your left hand. Boy, take his left hand and bring it near to my right. (JIM *does so.*) And now that's done.

BLIND PEW *taps out.* THE CAPTAIN *rises, shaking with fright, moves to centre of stage and slowly unclenches his left hand, at which he has not yet looked. There in his palm is* The Black Spot. THE CAPTAIN *looks at it with horror.*

CAPTAIN: The Black Spot! (THE CAPTAIN *clutches at his breast and falls.*) Jim, listen to me. They'll be back soon. That was the Black Spot they tipped me. But we'll beat 'em yet. They mustn't get Flint's fist. The chest, Jim boy, the chest (*pulling out key which is round his neck and pointing to his room*) and don't forget . . . beware the sea-faring man with one . . . leg.

THE CAPTAIN *has died. Enter* MRS. HAWKINS. *When she sees* THE CAPTAIN *she cries out.*

MRS. HAWKINS: Oh, Jim! Have they murdered him?

JIM: No, Mother. But he's dead. But, Mother, I thought you were going to the Squire's.

MRS. HAWKINS: I met Jim Hunter on his way home and he has run down with the message.

JIM: They'll be back soon, Mother. We haven't much time. They were after something in his sea chest.

MRS. HAWKINS: Maybe it was gold, Jim. Quick! Get the chest.

JIM exits. MRS. HAWKINS *locks door.* JIM *returns dragging chest. They open chest. It is empty save for some pistols, a telescope, a cutlass or two, a folded map and a bag of coins.*

MRS. HAWKINS *takes the bag to a table and empties it.*

Aha! I knew it! Gold!

BLIND PEW'S *stick is heard tapping and a rattle is heard as he tries the door. His tapping dies away.*

JIM: That was the blind man, Mother! Hurry! They'll be back in a minute.

MRS. HAWKINS: I'll show those rogues that I'm an honest woman. I'll have my due and not a penny more.

She counts coins. JIM *dashes to window.*

JIM: Hurry, Mother!

MRS. HAWKINS: These are all foreign coins. There's hardly a guinea here.

JIM: Well, take them all, Mother. It doesn't matter. Do please hurry.

MRS. HAWKINS: I'll not take any more than I am owed. Two blacks don't make a white.

She continues to sort the coins. JIM *dashes to the window again.*

JIM: Oh! Quick, Mother! They are coming up the hill. Out the back way! Take them all—it doesn't matter.

She does so and they exit hurriedly right. There is a short pause. Sounds are heard and the pirates burst in—BLIND PEW *followed by* TOM MORGAN *and* BLACK DOG. TOM MORGAN *sees* THE CAPTAIN's *body and dashes to it.*

MORGAN: Pew, Bill's dead.

PEW: Search him, you shirking lubber.

BLACK DOG: Look, Pew, the chest. They've been here before us. Someone has turned the chest up.

PEW: Is it there? Flint's fist, is it there?

BLACK DOG: Can't see it here nohow.

PEW: Is it on Bill, then?

MORGAN: Bill's been overhauled too. Nothing left.

PEW: It's the people of the inn. It's that boy. I wish I'd put his eyes out. They were here no time ago. They had the door bolted when I tried it. Scatter, lads, and find them. Rout the house out.

Exit BLACK DOG *right. Exit* TOM MORGAN *left. Noises off as they search the house.* PEW *moves about the room in a rage, stumbling over furniture. A whistle is heard in the distance. Enter* TOM MORGAN *and* BLACK DOG.

BLACK DOG: That's Dirk.

The whistle is heard twice.

MORGAN: That's Dirk again. Twice. We'll have to budge.

PEW: Budge? you skulk. Dirk's a fool and a coward.

They must be close by. Scatter and look for them. Oh, shiver m'soul, if I'd my eyes.

The others don't move but look at each other as if to say 'Let's go'.

You have your hands on thousands, you fools, and you hang a leg! You'd be as rich as kings if you could find it, and you know it's here, and you stand there malingering. There wasn't one of you dared face Bill, and I did it—a blind man! And I'm to lose my chance for you! I'm to be a poor crawling beggar, sponging for rum, when I might be rolling in a coach! If you had the pluck of a weevil in a biscuit you'd catch them still.

BLACK DOG: They might have hid the cursed thing. Let's get out of it, Pew. Don't stand there squalling.

PEW (*hysterically, striking about with his stick*): I'll not give them Flint's fist. I'll crawl no longer, blast ye.

BLACK DOG: Quick, come on.

Exit TOM MORGAN *and* BLACK DOG. PEW *suddenly stops.*

PEW: Dog, Tom, Dirk, you won't leave old Pew, boys, not old Pew.

Shouts in the distance. PEW, *in confusion, loses his bearings and stumbles about the room. Sounds of shooting.* PEW *is now up stage centre. Enter* JIM, *running, coming down stage left.*

JIM: This way, Squire. They've gone.

PEW *gives a cry.* JIM *turns round, sees him and stands rooted to the spot in terror.* PEW, *breathing heavily, slowly taps towards* JIM, *drawing a knife.* JIM *backs away to the table.*

PEW: You'll not cross Blind Pew again, my lad. No not you. Not when I've put your eyes out.

As he lunges forward DR. LIVESEY *appears at the doorway, pistol in hand, and shoots him. Enter* SQUIRE TRELAWNEY.

SQUIRE: Ah, Livesey, just in time, I see. Are you all right, Jim?

JIM: Yes, he didn't touch me.

SQUIRE (*turning to the door*): The rest of you scour the countryside. The villains cannot be far. They had no horses. Hurry now.

Off: Aye, Aye, sir, etc., etc. JIM *lights the lamp during the following dialogue.*

DR. LIVESEY: Well, Jim, do you know what the ruffians were after?

JIM: Yes, Doctor. A map belonging to someone called Flint. I have it here. It was in the Captain's sea chest.

SQUIRE: Flint? Flint, the pirate?

DR. LIVESEY: Then you have heard of him, Squire Trelawney?

SQUIRE: Heard of him. Heard of him, you say? He was the bloodthirstiest buccaneer that ever sailed. Blackbeard was a child to Flint. The Spaniards were so prodigiously afraid of him, that, I tell you, sir, I was sometimes proud he was an Englishman. I've seen his top-sails with these very eyes, off Trinidad, and the cowardly son of a rum-puncheon that I sailed with put back—put back, sir, into Port of Spain. But what do you make of that map, Livesey?

DR. LIVESEY: It seems to be the map of an island. See there's the latitude and there's the longtitude—and here

are some markings—Spyglass Mountain—South Hill—
and here's some crosses. Three of them. Unless I'm
very much mistaken, Squire, this map is of the island
where Captain Flint buried his famous treasure.

JIM: Treasure!

SQUIRE: Aye, Jim, treasure. Treasure worth a king's
ransom. For years Captain Flint sailed the Spanish
Main, sacking and murdering till his name was feared
in a hundred ports—and we have got the map. Livesey,
you will give up this wretched practice at once. Tomorrow I start for Bristol. In three weeks' time—three
weeks! two weeks—ten days—we'll have the best ship,
sir, and the choicest crew in England. Hawkins shall
come as cabin-boy. You'll make a famous cabin-boy,
Hawkins. You, Livesey, are ship's doctor; I am admiral.
We'll have favourable winds, a quick passage, and not
the least difficulty in finding the spot, and money to eat
—to roll in—to play duck and drake with ever after.

DR. LIVESEY: Trelawney, I'll go with you. And I'll go
bail for it; so will Jim, and be a credit to the under-
taking. There's only one man I'm afraid of.

SQUIRE: And who's that? Name the dog, sir!

DR. LIVESEY: You—for you cannot hold your tongue. We
are not the only men who know of this paper. These
fellows who attacked the inn tonight—bold, desperate
blades, for sure, and I dare say not far off—are, one and
all, through thick and thin, bound that they'll get that
money. We must none of us go alone till we get to sea.
Jim and I shall stick together in the meanwhile; you'll
take Joyce and Hunter when you ride to Bristol, and,
from first to last, not one of us must breathe a word of
what we've found.

SQUIRE: Livesey, you are always in the right of it. I'll be as silent as the grave. Come, let's take a last look around to make sure those scoundrels have really gone. (*Exit* DOCTOR *and* SQUIRE).

JIM (*his face shining*): Treasure! Doubloons! Guineas! Pieces of eight!

He draws an imaginary cutlass, leaps on to the table and sings.

> Fifteen men on the dead man's chest—
> Yo-ho-ho, and a bottle of rum!

CURTAIN

SCENE 2

The same as Scene One. Morning, two days later.
A FRIAR *in long robes and hood is seated at a table up right with his back to the audience. He is asleep. A wine bottle and glass and some dishes are on the table before him. Enter* JIM *carrying a basket of produce. He comes down left and puts down the basket. He turns, sees the* FRIAR, *and goes curiously to him. He has almost reached him when* MRS. HAWKINS *enters left.*

MRS. HAWKINS: Sshht! Jim, don't go waking the holy man up. He's had a long journey and he's very tired.

JIM: Sorry, Mother. I got the vegetables from Mr. Fisher.

MRS. HAWKINS: How much were they?

JIM: Fourpence, but he says if you send him a bottle of best whisky it will be all right.

Mrs. Hawkins: Well, now, isn't that nice of him! A bottle of best whisky is only threepence. (*Anxiously.*) You didn't see anything of any pirates down at the cove, did you?

Jim: No! They'll be too scared to come back here in a hurry. But, Mother? . . .

Mrs. Hawkins: Yes, Jim?

Jim: You haven't breathed a word to anyone, have you?

Mrs. Hawkins: Not a word, Jim. I've been too frightened even to think about it. Why, last night I had a most terrible nightmare.

Jim: Did you, Mother?

Mrs. Hawkins: Yes, Jim. I dreamed I was carried off by pirates and made to walk the plank, and there was hundreds of sharks waiting to gobble me up as soon as I fell. Then I got to the edge of the plank and was pushed.

Jim: Was that the end of the nightmare?

Mrs. Hawkins: The end! It was just the beginning! You see, I started swimming away from the sharks and they were—snap—snap—snapping at my heels.

Jim: But, Mother, you can't swim.

Mrs. Hawkins: I know, and, thank the Lord, just as I realised I couldn't I woke up.

Jim (*laughs*): Well, I'll go and peel the potatoes.

He picks up basket and exits left. Mrs. Hawkins *busies herself for the moment. Enter* Mrs. Trefuddle *and* Mrs. McGoo. *The former is extremely senile and very deaf; the latter, her daughter, is the village gossip.*

Mrs. McGoo: Good-day to you, Mrs. Hawkins.

Mrs. Hawkins. Good-day to you, Mrs. McGoo, good-day to you, Mrs. Trefuddle.

Mrs. McGoo: Mother just had to come over and talk to you as soon as she heard about your spot of bother the other night. (*They sit.*) Why, she hasn't stopped talking about it since. I tell you, I couldn't get a word in edgeways, could I, Mother?

Mrs. Trefuddle: Ahh? (Mrs. Trefuddle *invariably sounds like a sheep.*)

Mrs. McGoo: She said, 'I must go over to Mrs. Hawkins and ask her all about it.' Didn't you, Mother?

Mrs. Trefuddle: Ahh?

Mrs. Hawkins: Well, I'm not supposed to say a word about the map or the treasure, you see (*confidentially*) it's a secret.

Mrs. McGoo: Treasure! Oh, you must tell me all about it. We are dying to hear, aren't we, Mother?

Mrs. Trefuddle: Ahh?

Mrs. Hawkins: Well, I really oughtn't to, but if you promise you won't tell a soul. . . .

Mrs. McGoo: Not a word—I promise you.

Mrs. Hawkins: Oh, very well, then. It was like this: The night before last we was sitting here minding our own business when without so much as a word of warning a gang of the most villainous cut-throats descended on the inn. There was at least twenty. Luckily, the door was bolted and all thirty of them was rattling at the door enough to scare the very soul from your body.

Mrs. McGoo: What a terrible thing. Did you hear that, Mother?

Mrs. Trefuddle: Ahh?

Mrs. McGoo: Tell me, Mrs. Hawkins, whatever did you do?

Mrs. Hawkins: Well, Jim got down the Captain's sea chest, the poor Captain, God rest his soul had died of fright and his last words to us were, 'God bless you, Mrs. Hawkins, and help yourself to anything you may find in my sea chest'—and what do you think we found in the chest?

Mrs. McGoo: What?

Mrs. Hawkins: A map showing where to find buried treasure.

Mrs. McGoo: Did you hear that, Mother? Treasure!

Mrs. Trefuddle: Ahh?

Mrs. Hawkins: And guess whose treasure do you think it is?

Mrs. McGoo: Whose?

Mrs. Hawkins: The famous Captain Flint!

Mrs. McGoo: Well, I never! Did you hear that, Mother? Captain Flint!

Mrs. Trefuddle: Ah-h!

Mrs. McGoo: What did you do with the map?

Mrs. Hawkins: The Squire and the Doctor looked at it and they decided to sail for the island and find the treasure—and guess what? Jim's to go as cabin boy! The Squire went to Bristol yesterday to buy a ship and they'll be sailing within the month.

Mrs. McGoo: Well, I do declare! I never heard anything so amazing in all my life.

Mrs. Hawkins: Of course, you won't breathe a word to anyone, will you? Because if any of the pirates got to hear of it, they might splice their mainbraces or something.

Mrs. McGoo: Why, I wouldn't dream of saying a word—and I'll make sure Mother doesn't either. You know how her tongue always wags. (*To* Mrs. Trefuddle.) Don't it, Mother?

Mrs. Trefuddle: Ah-h?

Mrs. McGoo: Now, we really ought to be going. I've all my baking to do. (*Rising.*) Come along, Mother.

Mrs. Hawkins (*showing them to the door*): Good-bye, Mrs. McGoo. Good-bye, Mrs. Trefuddle. It's been so nice to see you.

Mrs. McGoo: It's been nice seeing you too. Mother does love to get out and *talk* to people—don't you, Mother?

Mrs. Trefuddle: A-h-h.

Mrs. Trefuddle *and* Mrs. McGoo *exit.* Mrs. Hawkins *watches them through the door for a second or two and then exits left. There is a pause and the* Friar *raises his head, places a few coins on the table and picking up his crutch, which has up to now remained unseen, he slowly moves to the door. It is seen that he has but one leg. As he reaches the door . . .*

THE CURTAIN FALLS

Scene 3

The same, two weeks later. Jim *is discovered right, wiping table.* Mrs. Hawkins *seated left, peeling potatoes.*

Enter Dr. Livesey. *'Good-mornings' all round.*

Dr. Livesey: Well, Jim, are you all packed for our voyage to 'Treasure Island'?

Mrs. Hawkins: Packed! He's been packed these two weeks. Not a minute's peace I've had. Him and his Treasure Island. I'm sure you will all be murdered in your beds—every man jack of you.

Jim: Not beds, Mother, hammocks. Sailors don't have beds. And anyway, Squire says I'm to have a cutlass and maybe even a pistol.

Dr. Livesey: I shouldn't count your chickens, Jim. I have had a letter from the Squire yesterday, from Bristol. He is having great trouble in finding a crew.

Jim: But why? I would've thought there would have been hundreds willing to sail and look for treasure.

Dr. Livesey: That's just it, Jim. If we let it be known that we were sailing for treasure, we might ship all sorts of ruffians, maybe even pirates in disguise, who would let us sail to the island and then mutiny on us. So we are going to sail under *Sealed Orders*. No one will know where we are going until we have set sail, except the Captain. And unfortunately there are not many men willing to sail under Sealed Orders. However, we've got a ship—the Squire bought her last week. She is called the *Hispaniola*, and a fine ship she is by all accounts. But the Squire will be here himself today and he will tell you all about it.

Mrs. Hawkins: Well, I had best be about the chores. I can't stand here gossiping to you old salts all day. (*Exit, laughing.*)

Jim: What happens, Doctor, if we can't find a crew? Does that mean we won't be able to sail after all?

Dr. Livesey: Oh, don't worry, Jim. Something will turn up.

The sound of a horse, off. Jim *goes to the window.*

Jim: Why, it's the Squire—here from Bristol, already.

Enter Squire.

Squire: Ah! Livesey, my dear fellow. Jim, my boy. Great news! I have a crew.

Jim: A crew?

Dr. Livesey: Excellent, my dear fellow. How did you find them?

Squire: By an amazing stroke of luck. There I was on the quayside, feeling very despondent. True, I had just found a fine captain. Smollett is his name. But, what good is a ship, I said to myself, with just a captain and a cabin boy, eh, Jim?

Jim *springs to attention and salutes.*

Jim: Aye, Aye, Admiral.

Squire: Well, as I said, there I was on the quayside, when by the merest accident I fell to talking with an old salt who kept a public-house and knew all the sea-faring men in Bristol. He, himself, was tired of being a publican and wanted to get a good berth as cook to go to sea again, and he had only that morning hobbled down to the quayside to get a smell of the sea. (*Expressions of sympathy from* JIM *and the* DOCTOR.) I was monstrously touched. So would you have been, and out of pure pity I engaged him on the spot to be ship's cook. Long John Silver he is called and he has lost a leg, but that I regard as a recommendation since he lost it in his country's service under the immortal Hawke.

DR. LIVESEY: Yes, Squire, but he is a cook and you said you had found a crew.

SQUIRE: Well, sir, I thought I had only found a cook, but it *was* a crew I had discovered. Between Silver and myself we got together in the space of a day a company of the toughest old salts imaginable. Not pretty to look at, but fellows, by their faces, of the most indomitable spirit. I declare we could fight a frigate.

DR. LIVESEY: I hope we never have to do that.

SQUIRE: Long John even got rid of two men I myself engaged. He showed me in a moment that they were just the sort of freshwater swabs we had to fear in an adventure of importance.

JIM (*unable to contain himself*): Tell me, Squire, when do we sail?

SQUIRE: Sail? Why, the day after tomorrow. And now, Livesey, I found in Bristol a most remarkable bottle of old brandy. You must share it with me over dinner tonight.

DR. LIVESEY: Gladly.

SQUIRE (*turning at the door*): Oh, by the way, Jim, I forgot to tell you—Long John Silver, having sold his public-house, was in need of lodgings for a day or two. I told him he could stay here until we sail. He will be arriving any minute, I passed him in the village on my way here.

JIM: Aye, aye, sir. I'll tell Mother.

Exit SQUIRE *and* DOCTOR. JIM *picks up a tray and exits left.*

SILVER (*off*): This is the place. The h-Admiral Benbow h-inn. Just the place to spend a night or two, eh, Tom?

MORGAN (*off*): Aye, 'tis that.

Enter LONG JOHN SILVER. *He stands for a moment in the doorway. He is dressed as a seaman and has only one leg. Under his left arm is a crutch. With the aid of which he hops about, bird-like fashion. He looks a likeable man and is about fifty years of age. He enters followed by* TOM MORGAN.

SILVER: Hallo, there! Is there anyone aboard?

Enter JIM.

JIM: Good-day, sirs. (*Stops on seeing* SILVER.) Why, sir, the Squire told me to expect you, that is, if you are Mr. Silver.

SILVER: Aye, that I am, matey. They call me Long John. Long John Silver, on account of I lost a leg in the service of the King, and this is my old shipmate, Tom Morgan. As fine a fo'c'sle hand as ever sailed the Spanish M . . . er . . . Seven Seas.

JIM: How do you do, sir. Squire said you would stay with us until you sailed.

SILVER: Aye, that we will. This is a very pleasant spot. (*They sit.*) Tell me, Jim, you're sailing with us, aren't you?

JIM: Yes, sir—as cabin boy.

SILVER: Have you ever been to sea before?

JIM: No, sir.

SILVER: Aha! Well, you've picked a good man to teach you. Long John Silver won't steer you wrong, lad.

JIM: Do you think we might run into any pirates?

SILVER (*innocently*): Pirates, Jim? What made you think of pirates? I don't expect we shall run into any pirates, do you, Tom?

MORGAN (*with exaggerated innocence*): N-o-o.

SILVER: N-o-o-o.

MORGAN (*shaking head violently*): N-o-o-o-o.

SILVER: Mind you, if we do, there's none better in a fight that Long John Silver. Many's the time I defended His Majesty's ships against those gentlemen of fortune, as they call themselves. Why, I've even had a brush with the famous Captain Flint. (*At the mention of 'Flint', JIM starts.*) Have you heard tell of Flint, Jim?

JIM: Yes, I think so.

SILVER: A bloodthirsty pirate he was, Jim. A scourge to the King's ships—God bless King George! Well, he's dead, thank the Lord, and me and my mates can handle any of these young upstarts like Henry Morgan and suchlike. And now, Jim, would you be getting us a wee drop of rum? Not that I'm a drinking man, mind you, but a little to warm the innards after the journey.

JIM: Yes, Mr. Silver. (*Exits.*)

MORGAN: I don't like that boy. He may have been hanging around that night and seen me.

SILVER: Not on your life, Tom, my boy. He's an innercent as a new-born babe. You've only to look at his face.

MORGAN: All the same, I don't like it.

Enter MRS. HAWKINS, *carrying rum.*

MRS. HAWKINS: Good-day, sirs.

SILVER AND MORGAN: Good-day, ma'am.

MRS. HAWKINS *puts down tray.*

MRS. HAWKINS: You'ld be Mr. Silver, sir, and you'ld be Mr. Morgan?

SILVER: That's right, ma'am. I see the lad has spoken to you. Don't tell me—let me guess—you're his mother!

MRS. HAWKINS: Indeed I am, and not a minute's peace have I had since his head was filled with all this talk of buccaneers, and cut-throats and the like. You're sailing with him on the *Hispaniola*, aren't you?

SILVER: Why, yes, ma'am. I'm ship's cook, and Tom here is fo'c'sle hand.

MRS. HAWKINS *brightens up considerably and starts to speak at breakneck speed.*

MRS. HAWKINS: Ship's cook! Why, then, you are just the man I want to see. Now, firstly, every night before going to bed you must give him a glass of hot milk . . .

LONG JOHN SILVER *opens his mouth to speak here and throughout her speech, but cannot succeed in interrupting.*

. . . with just a little piece of butter in it if the weather is cold, and if his tummy should get upset in all that horrible rough weather, be sure he has some nice gruel . . .

. . . not, of course, that he likes gruel, but it's good for him, I know. Now, as to the things he does like—he is very fond of plum pudding, roast turkey, chicken . . .

. . . but only the white meat, jam tarts, apples, pears, roast beef and yorkshire pudding and candied orange rind . . .

. . . and he *doesn't* like, fish, milk puddings, soft-boiled eggs, fatty bacon and lettuce . . .

. . . and of course spinnach. Spinnach—always—makes—him—sick . . .

. . . there, you won't forget any of that, will you?

LONG JOHN SILVER *and* TOM MORGAN *having by now been stunned into silence shake their heads very slowly in unison.*

MRS. HAWKINS *exits.*

SILVER (*hoarsely*): No matter what 'appens—sharks, doldrums, fever, earthquakes, I'll be thankful for one thing.

MORGAN: What's that?

SILVER: That it's Jim Hawkins that's coming with us, and not his mum!

MORGAN: I'd just as soon cut her throat as his.

SILVER (*banging table*): I'll have none of your talk of throat-cutting, Tom Morgan. You always was an ignorant swab, and your years ashore ain't improved you none.

MORGAN: Well, aren't we going to cut their throats?

SILVER: Aye, but when I gives the word and not before.

MORGAN: The men won't like that, John. They be planning on the first night out at sea.

SILVER: I'll take care of the men. I can handle Flint's old crew. There were some that was feared of Pew and some that was feared of Flint, but Flint himself was feared of me, feared he was and proud. They was the roughest crew afloat, was Flint's. The devil himself would've been feared to go to sea with them. I'm not a boasting man, but I'll tell you—when I was quartermaster, *lambs* wasn't the word for Flint's old buccaneers.

Enter JIM.

JIM: Mr. Silver?

SILVER: Yes, Jim?

JIM: Could I ask you a favour?

SILVER: Yes, Jim, my boy. What is it?

JIM: Well, Squire said I was to have a cutlass and maybe even a pistol. But I've never used a cutlass and I thought that perhaps you might—well—sort of teach me.

SILVER: Teach you! Aye, and gladly, lad. Why, before me wings was clipped there was nary a finer cutlass man aboard in all . . . the King's ships. (*Standing.*) Many's the buccaneer I've cut down in the Spanish Main. Why, one day, there we was, a week out of Maracaibo, and all of a sudden the lookout yells, 'Sail on the starb'd beam', and Admiral Hawke he ups with his spyglass and he has a look. 'Silver,' he says to me, 'that's Blackbeard's ship.' 'Aye, sir, it is that,' I says. 'Silver,' he says, 'shall we run or shall we fight?' 'Run, sir,' I says, 'in a King's ship! Never! Never!' I says, 'We'll fight, sir,' I says. 'Silver, you're right,' says the Admiral. So we trimmed sail and ran for him. We got nearer and nearer. As soon as we got in his range he let fire with his guns. We replied. And that's the way it goes—bang, bang, bang—and all the time we got closer and closer and closer. Then I sees Blackbeard's men standing by with the grappling irons. 'Stand by to repel boarders,' I yells, and then . . . we met.

JIM (*breathlessly*): What happened?

SILVER: Why, we fought for four hours. Tom Morgan, here he got nine, and I killed fourteen including the great Blackbeard himself. The decks was running with blood.

JIM: Gosh!

SILVER: So you see there's none better to teach you the cutlass than Old Long John himself. Be square with me and you'll find that no man or boy has a better friend than Long John Silver.

SILVER *starts to sit down. As he does so* MRS. HAWKINS *enters, beginning to speak to him. He rises immediately, as does* TOM MORGAN, *apprehensive looks on their faces.*

SILVER: Beggin' your pardon, ma'am, but me and Tom'll just stroll down to the village to stretch our legs. Shan't be long. Now remember, Jim, be a good lad and do all your mother says.

Exit MORGAN *and* SILVER.

MRS. HAWKINS: You know, Jim, I *do* like that Mr. Silver.

JIM: Do you, Mother? So do I!

MRS. HAWKINS: Yes. He's such a *nice* man.

CURTAIN

ACT II

SCENE 1

Some weeks later. The deck of the Hispaniola *approaching Treasure Island. The bow of the ship is off stage right. The stern is off stage left. There is a large barrel somewhere or other.* LONG JOHN SILVER *is seated on a stool mixing something in a basin. Enter* JIM *with a packet of salt.*

JIM: Here's the salt, Mr. Silver.

SILVER: Thank you, Jim me boy. It was kind of you to save my old legs, I mean leg.

JIM: It's a pleasure, Mr. Silver. I enjoy helping about the ship. There's so much to learn, isn't there?

SILVER: That there is, lad, that there is. I well remember when I was a lad making some terrible mistakes.

JIM: Mr. Silver.

SILVER: Yes, Jim.

JIM: Are there many pirates in these waters?

SILVER: Hundreds probably, why?

JIM: Because I'd like us to be *attacked*.

SILVER: Now why on earth should you be wanting that?

JIM: So that I can see how much I've learnt about cutlass fighting.

SILVER: You don't want to be bothered about warlike things like that, Jim. We peaceable men have got to think of other things.

JIM (*with a sigh*): Yes, I suppose so.

SILVER: Now; how's your hornpipe getting on?

JIM (*brightening*): Jolly good. I've been practising quite hard.

SILVER: Right, lad, we'll get you some music. Tom! Bosun Smith! Dead Bones! Up on deck! Now we'll see how much of a sailor you are.

Enter TOM MORGAN, BOSUN SMITH, *and* DEAD BONES JONES, *during following speech.* 'BOSUN SMITH' *is* BLACK DOG *with a beard.*

Every sailor knows how to hornpipe. Why, before I lost my pin I was the best hornpiper in all the King's Fleet. Now then . . . (*he names whichever* PIRATE *plays the recorder*) out with your clarionet, and pipe up.

The PIRATE *pipes and* JIM *hornpipes. The* PIRATES *have been rather bored with all this and are now quite surly. As* JIM *finishes* BLACK DOG *turns to* SILVER.

BLACK DOG: Was there anything else, *Mr.* Silver?

SILVER: Now you comes to mention it, 'Bosun Smith', there was. I've just been telling Jim here that every good sailor can do a hornpipe, so hows about you lot giving us all a demingstration?

JONES (*unutterably amazed*): *Wot!*

SILVER: You 'eard me, Dead Bones.

BLACK DOG: You'll not get me to . . .

SILVER: You'll 'ornpipe, and you, Tom, and you, Dead Bones. And what's more, you'll like it. (SILVER *takes the recorder. The* PIRATES *give him appropriate looks.* SILVER *puts the recorder to his mouth, and then, as an idea strikes him, takes it away.*) And you'll sing. (*The* PIRATES *start to protest.*) Because if you don't you'll get no supper tonight, and it's pork pie—(*the* PIRATES *soften a little*) with gravy—(*the* PIRATES *soften even more*) and treacle tart—(*the* PIRATES *lick their lips*) and—(*the* PIRATES *hang on his next words*) custard. (*The* PIRATES *breathe sighs of relief. Obviously it is their dream of heaven.*) Now then, are you ready?

MORGAN: What shall we sing?

SILVER: Een hodi krai palekomos nautees.

BLACK DOG: What's that?

SILVER: That's Greek for, 'What shall we do with the drunken sailor'.

BLACK DOG: Oh.

SILVER *plays the recorder and the* PIRATES *sing and dance to the 'Drunken Sailor' grudgingly. At the finish* SILVER *and* JIM *laugh.*

SILVER: Thank you, lads. That was very nice.

Exit PIRATES.

Help me up, Jim lad, and I'll set about making that tart.

JIM *helps* SILVER *off. Enter left* SQUIRE TRELAWNEY, DR. LIVESEY *and* CAPTAIN SMOLLETT. SMOLLETT *is a stern well-dressed sailor of about forty.*

SQUIRE: Well, the men are certainly in good spirits today, eh, Captain Smollett?

SMOLLETT (*noncommitally*): Aye, sir, they are.

SQUIRE: And rightly so. It's a good thing.

SMOLLETT: That depends, sir, on whether you like a crew in good spirits.

SQUIRE: Why not? I like to see men happy, and they should be happy. Fair winds, fair weather, and a double ration of rum. What more can a crew ask?

SMOLLETT: If you ask me, Squire, we pander to them too much. It doesn't do to be too easy on a crew. Double rum, short watches, and a barrel of apples on deck for every man-jack to help himself to whenever he feels like it. Still, they've done their work well, I'll say that for them. From the look of them I didn't think they would.

DR. LIVESEY: Yes, they've been as good as gold.

SMOLLETT (*to himself*): Perhaps a little too good.

DR. LIVESEY: What's that, Smollett?

SMOLLETT: Nothing.

They have been walking slowly across the deck. They are now down stage right. Enter JIM, *carrying polished frying pan.*

DR. LIVESEY: Ah! Jim. Looking forward to seeing your fabulous island?

JIM: Yes, sir. (*In a whisper, glancing over his shoulder.*) Are we nearly there?

DR. LIVESEY: Captain Smollett seems to think we will sight land today or perhaps tomorrow.

JIM (*excitedly*): Oh, good!

SQUIRE: He's quite a sailor now, isn't he, Livesey? I didn't think he would be—he was that sick the first day out, eh? (*Starts to laugh.*)

DR. LIVESEY (*joining in the laughter*): No, I didn't think he would be either. Do you remember that time he spat into the wind?

Squire (*laughing more*): Yes.

Dr. Livesey (*laughing even more*): And you were standing next to him?

Squire (*suddenly stops laughing*): Most uncalled for, Livesey, most uncalled for.

Smollett: Tell me, Jim—you live with the crew and you know them pretty well. Have they any inkling of why we have sailed? Has any news about Treasure Island leaked out?

Jim: I don't think so, sir. I've not heard any of the hands mention it.

Squire: Oh, I don't think it matters now. They're all good lads. We should get no trouble from any of them.

Dr. Livesey: Besides, Smollett, we will have to tell them sooner or later since we will need their help to dig for the treasure and to get it aboard the ship.

Smollett (*doubtfully*): Yes, I suppose so.

Dr. Livesey: Well, we can tell them after we sight land.

Squire: Yes, yes, of course. Let's go and have another look at the map. (*As they go out.*) Oh, Jim, if there are any apples left in the barrel, you might bring some along to the cabin, will you? I am feeling a little peckish.

Exit left, Squire, Dr. Livesey *and* Captain Smollett. Jim *goes to the barrel, bends over it but cannot reach the apples which are at the bottom. He steps on a box which is lying alongside of the barrel and gets in. As his head disappears, enter right*, Long John Silver, Tom Morgan *and* Black Dog.

BLACK DOG: I say do it now, while they ain't expecting it.

SILVER: No point at all, Black Dog. If they ain't expecting it now, they'll never be expecting it, will they? You listen to Long John Silver. He'll not steer you wrong.

BLACK DOG: I've been listening to you long enough, and look where it landed me!—with a beard! I can't sleep o' nights for scratching, I can't.

MORGAN: Well, you wants to wash yourself, Dog. I bet there's more fleas in your beard than in Long John's breeches.

TOM MORGAN *laughs.* LONG JOHN *silences him with a look.*

SILVER: Well, I've not steered you wrong yet. Just have a little patience.

MORGAN: Still, I'm tired, Long John, of living in the fo'c'sle and having me rum doled out to me like a babe in arms. I wants to get into that cabin, I do. I wants their pickles and wines.

SILVER: Tom, your head ain't of much account, nor never was, but you're able to hear I reckon—leastways your ears is big enough. Now, here's what I say. You'll berth for'ard and you'll live hard and you'll speak soft and you'll keep sober until I give the word.

MORGAN: What I want to know is—when? When are you going to give the word?

SILVER: When, by the Powers! Well, now, if you want to know I'll tell you when. The last moment I can manage; and that's when. Here's a first-rate seaman, Captain Smollett, sails the blessed ship for us. Here's the Squire and the Doctor with the map—I don't know where it is, do I? No more do you. Well, then, I mean this

Squire and Doctor to find the stuff and help us to get it aboard. Then we'll see. If I was sure of you and the rest of the crew I'd have Captain Smollett navigate us half-way back again before I struck.

BLACK DOG: Why? We're all seamen aboard.

SILVER: We're all fo'c'sle hands you mean. We can stear a course but who's going to set one? That's what all you gentlemen split on first and last. If I'd my way, I'd have Captain Smollett work us back into the Trades at least. Then we'd have no blessed miscalculations and a spoonful of water a day. But I know the sort you lot are—hurryguts all of you.

MORGAN: Easy, John! You've no reason to be calling us names.

SILVER: How many tall ships d'you think I've seen laid aboard, and how many brisk lads hanging in chains and drying in the sun on Execution Dock?—and all for the same reason—hurry, hurry, hurry.

BLACK DOG: Aye, but we've all been gentlemen of fortune long enough and stayed alive too. You're no better than the rest of us, Long John, quartermaster or no quartermaster. We all sailed with Flint, same as you.

SILVER: Oho! And where are Flint's crew now? Pew—he was your sort and he died a beggarman. Flint died of rum at Savannah, and Bones of the same disease too. And the rest of Flint's merry men—aboard here and glad to get the duff—most of 'em were begging and starving ashore. No, lads, we'll wait.

BLACK DOG: 'Taint good enough, Long John. We all talked it over last night and we came to a decision—a *majority* decision. We're going to get that map as soon as the land is sighted, and take our chance on navigating back. Why, they might even get the treasure aboard and maroon us on the island.

SILVER: Never, never, while I'm captain.

MORGAN: Well, the men are down below. You'd best talk to them yourself. They're in an ugly mood.

SILVER (*draws cutlass*): Talk to them! I'll talk to the yellow-bellied, white-livered, weevil-legged, scabby sons of landlubbers!

Exit LONG JOHN *followed by* BLACK DOG *and* TOM MORGAN *right.* JIM's *head appears above the rim of the barrel. He looks about him and clambers out. As he does so, the* SQUIRE, DR. LIVESEY *and* CAPTAIN SMOLLETT *enter.*

JIM: Squire! Squire!

SQUIRE: What is it, Jim? You look scared to death.

JIM: They're pirates—all of them!

SQUIRE: What!!

JIM: The crew! Long John Silver! Tom Morgan and Bosun Smith, but his name's not really Bosun Smith, it's Black Dog and he's grown a beard. And all the rest of the crew—they're all Captain Flint's old crew and they plan to murder us all as soon as the island is sighted—and they know about the map!

SMOLLETT: How do you know all this, lad? Quick, speak up.

JIM: I had to get inside the apple barrel to get the apples out because they were all at the bottom and Long John walked by with Morgan and Bosun Smith—er—Black Dog, and I heard them talking. I heard the whole thing.

Squire: What an ass I am for trusting them so.

Smollett: No more of an ass than I, sir. I never heard of a crew that meant to mutiny and showed no signs before. But this crew beats me.

Dr. Livesey: That's Silver's doing, Captain. A very remarkable man.

Smollett: He would look remarkably well hanging from a yardarm, sir. But this is just talk. It doesn't lead anywhere. We have to make a plan. They will probably demand the map and then leave us aboard with guards while they go ashore to find the treasure. As soon as they find it they will cut our throats. Now, as I see it, we must make plans to escape whilst they are on the island looking for the treasure.

Dr. Livesey: But how can we do that? They will disarm us, surely?

Jim: I have an idea, Captain!

Smollett: What's that?

Jim: Well, all the pistols and powder and shot are in the Powder Room. You remember you gave orders at the beginning of the voyage. Well, if I can sneak into the Powder Room and get some pistols, powder and shot and hide them under the floorboards in your cabin, we can escape later.

Squire: Do you think you could do it, Jim? It's right by the crew's quarters.

Jim: I'll try, Squire.

Squire: Good lad! Off you go!

Exit Jim *right.*

Smollett: That's a brave lad, Squire.

DR. LIVESEY: He'll have to be more than brave for this job. He'll have to be clever too, for there's no denying, Captain, that at the present moment it is on Jim Hawkins that our lives depend.

Voice off: Land ho! Land on the starboard beam!

SMOLLETT (*gazing through telescope*): He made his discovery not a moment too soon.

DR. LIVESEY: Is it the island?

SMOLLETT: Definitely.

SQUIRE: Are you sure?

SMOLLETT: Positive. I recognise it from the chart. I can see Spyglass Mountain, and there's the harbour. It looks quite deserted.

DR. LIVESEY: There probably hasn't been a soul on it for years. We're miles off any of the normal sea routes.

SQUIRE: Here, let me have a look. Yes, it's a wonderful sight. If we had an honest crew with us this would be the happiest day of my life.

SMOLLETT: I hope Jim is successful, for if he isn't it will be the last day of your life.

SQUIRE: Don't be so damned depressing. We'll win through yet.

The three men are now facing down stage left. Enter SILVER, TOM MORGAN, BLACK DOG *and* DEAD BONES JONES, *with drawn cutlasses.*

SILVER: Captain!

They turn.

SMOLLETT: What is the meaning of this, Silver? Get those men below and put away those cutlasses.

SILVER: Begging your pardon, Captain, no!

SMOLLETT: Mr. Silver—this is mutiny.

SILVER: Begging your pardon, Captain, and what if it is?

SMOLLETT: You'll not get away with this, Silver. You'll be hanged—every man jack of you.

JONES: You'll not live to see the day.

SILVER: Leave this to me, Dead Bones. I'm in charge of this here mutiny. Now, gentlemen, I don't have to tell you what we've come about.

DR. LIVESEY: I don't know what you mean, and I warn you that if you . . .

SILVER: You're in no position to warn anyone, Doctor. I'm the Master here now.

BLACK DOG: We're wasting time, Long John. Let's slit their throats and have done with it.

SILVER: Quiet, fungus-face. Now, Squire, Doctor, Captain—you've got something that belongs to us.

SQUIRE: Not that I am aware of, my good man.

SILVER: Come, come, Squire! Ain't you being a little forgetful? (*His manner suddenly changing.*) It's Flint's fist I'm speaking about and if it's not in my hand this minute you'll all walk the plank.

JIM *enters left, whistling unconcernedly. He stops on seeing the* PIRATES *and feigns surprise.*

SILVER: You can join your friends, Jim Hawkins, since you're the cause of all their trouble. Now, Squire—the map.

DR. LIVESEY: And if we give you the map, Silver, not that I'm saying we will, but if we do, what then?

SILVER (*all smiles*): Why then, Doctor, we shall be most happy to set you and your friends quite free to roam your Treasure Island at will, looking for any pieces of eight that me and my lads may have missed. (*The* PIRATES *laugh*.) With, of course, provisions to last you a month or two. And, as a special favour, we'll stop the first ship we sight coming this way and tell them to pick you up. The only other alternative is that we slit your throats here and now and take a chance of finding the map ourselves, or just digging until we find the treasure. And if you're thinking of fighting your way out of this, Captain Smollett, you've another think coming, for two of me boys is sitting outside the Powder Room with loaded pistols.

SMOLLETT: It doesn't seem that we have much choice. What do you say, Squire?

SQUIRE: I agree.

SILVER: Well, now, that's real matey of you. And just to make sure you don't try any funny business while we're ashore, we'll take young Jim 'ere as a sort of 'ostage like. And now how about our little map?

SQUIRE: You know where the map is, Jim. Go and get it.

SILVER: Hurry along there, Jim. Don't keep your old pal waiting.

Exit JIM *left*. BLACK DOG *beckons* LONG JOHN *aside*.

BLACK DOG: Why don't we cut their throats now, Long John, and have done with it?

SILVER: Oh, Dog, you're that stupid sometimes, I feel real sorry for you. Supposing they tried some trickery and gave us a faked map. Then where would we be? A ship with no treasure, no captain, nothing. We'll wait until we've got the treasure and then ... (*he makes a sign of cutting a throat.*)

Enter Jim, *carrying map. He gives the map to* Long John Silver.

Silver: This is it! Flint's fist! Israel! Israel Hands!

Voice off: Aye, Long John?

Silver: You and George Merry lower a longboat and then stand by to stay as guards while we go ashore.

Voice off: Aye, aye.

Silver: Right, lads! Now for the treasure! You'll come with me, Jim Hawkins. And you gentlemen will presently be locked in your cabin. In the meantime, if you try and leave this quarterdeck, me lads'll have to cut you down, which would be a terrible sad thing, would it not? Come, lads.

Exit Pirates *with* Jim.

Squire: We're in a tricky position, Smollett. We can't fight our guards with young Jim as a hostage. At the first shot the scoundrels would cut his throat.

Smollett: I know! I know something else, too, Squire —that as soon as they have found the treasure they'll be back here, knives in hand to cut *our* throats.

Squire: But Silver gave his word.

Smollett: His word! What do you think his word means to a man like Silver? He daren't leave us alive when he knows that the minute we reach England we could have him hanged. No, sir! We have no option but to escape, and to take a chance on Silver sparing Jim. For, if we don't escape, and quickly too, as sure as God made little apples, we'll end up in Davy Jones's locker.

Dr. Livesey: I'm afraid he's right, Squire. Smollett, lend me your spyglass. The longboat's approaching the island. Ah, there it is. There's Jim sitting up in the bows. And there's that rascal, Silver, in the stern, waving his crutch like one of those new-fangled cricket bats.

Squire: How long do you think it will take them to find the treasure?

Smollett. Well, it'll be dark in an hour, so there is not much of a start they can get tonight, but if they get an early start in the morning, they may have located it by noon tomorrow.

Dr. Livesey: They're just pulling into the beach. (*Excitedly.*) Jim's jumped! He's making for the forest. Why, he's running like a hare. There's three of them after him.

Squire: Run! Jim, run!

Smollett: Go it, lad! Go it, lad!

Dr. Livesey: He's made it. They'll never find him in there. Silver's beckoning them back. They're not following him.

Squire: That means that we can use the pistols.

Smollett: Yes, but not before morning. If we attempted to land on the island at night we might run into an ambush.

Dr. Livesey: I don't like the idea of that lad being alone all night with those scoundrels roaming around.

Smollett: I shouldn't worry too much about him, Doctor. Silver and his cut-throats will probably be too full of rum before long to harm anybody, and the lad's got great courage.

SQUIRE: He has that. If I had some wine, gentlemen, I'd toast his health.

DR. LIVESEY: Let's do it then—with or without wine, the wish is the same. (*They clink imaginary glasses.*)

ALL: Jim Hawkins!

CURTAIN

SCENE 2

Dawn the next morning.

A clearing on the island. JIM *is asleep slightly right of down stage centre. Jungle noises are heard, and as the sun comes over Spyglass Mountain, the clearing is fully illuminated.*

BEN GUNN *appears left. He is a small gaunt individual with flowing white hair and beard. He is dressed in rags and moves more like an ape than a man. He speaks in a high-pitched voice. He scurries up to* JIM *and peers at him.* JIM *wakes and sits up.* BEN *darts behind a tree.* JIM *stretches, yawns.* BEN GUNN *enters again, comes forward and throws himself on his knees in front of* JIM. JIM *jumps back, afraid.*

JIM: W-who are you?

BEN: I'm poor Ben Gunn, I am, and I haven't spoke with a Christian these three years.

JIM: Three years! Were you shipwrecked?

BEN: No, mate. Marooned. Marooned three years agone.

And I've lived on goats since then, and berries and oysters. Wherever a man is, says I, a man can do for himself. But mate, my heart is sore for Christian diet. You mightn't happen to have a piece of cheese about you, now?

JIM: I'm terribly sorry, Mr. Gunn, but I haven't any cheese on me. As a matter of fact I'm very hungry myself.

BEN: Well, many's the long night I've dreamed of cheese —toasted mostly—and woke up again and, here I was.

JIM: If ever I get aboard again you shall have cheese by the stone.

BEN: If ever you get aboard again, says you. Why, now, who's to hinder you?

JIM: Not you, I know.

BEN: And right you is. Now, young matey, what do you call yourself?

JIM: My name's Jim. Jim Hawkins.

BEN: Jim. Jim. Jim. Jim. Jim. (*He tries it up and down the scale.*) Well now, Jim. I've lived that rough as you'd be ashamed to hear of. Now, for instance, you wouldn't think I had a pious mother—not to look at me?

JIM: Well, if you don't mind my saying so, Mr. Gunn, I wouldn't.

BEN: Ah well, but I had!—*re*markable pious! And I was a good-mannered pious boy, and could rattle off the Lord's prayer so fast, so's you couldn't tell one word from another. And now, now I come to this. (*He breaks down and sobs.*)

JIM: Please don't cry, Mr. Gunn. I'm sure things aren't as bad as they seem.

BEN (*sobbing even harder*): It's no use comforting me, Jim. I'm past comforting. I got my just deserts, I did. I was wicked.

JIM: Oh, surely not.

BEN: Yes, I was. It's me wickedness that brought it on, Jim, but I thought it all out on this lonely island, and I'm going back to piety. I'll never drink rum again——well, just a thimbleful for luck, of course, the first chance I get. But mark my words, I'll be as good as gold. (*He claps his hand to his mouth.*) There! I've said it.

JIM: Said what, Mr. Gunn?

GUNN *looks all round him, puts his arm round* JIM *and moves him a little way from where they are standing. He opens his mouth to speak and then repeats the performance.*

Said what, Mr. Gunn?

BEN: Gold.

JIM (*blankly*): Oh!

BEN: Jim, boy, I'm rich—rich as Midas, and I'll tell you what—I'll make you rich too. You'll bless your stars, Jim Hawkins, that you was the first that found me.

JIM: Thank you very much, Mr. Gunn.

BEN (*suddenly anxious*): Now, Jim, tell me true, that ain't Flint's ship out there, is it?

JIM: It's not Flint's ship, and Flint is dead; but I'll tell you true as you ask me, there are some of Flint's old crew aboard, worse luck for the rest of us.

BEN: Not a man with—with—one leg?

JIM: Do you mean Long John Silver?

At the sound of SILVER's *name,* GUNN *leaps into the air with a shriek, then rushes at* JIM *and grabs him.*

BEN: Was you sent by Long John? (*Shakes him.*) Was you?

JIM: No, I'm running away from Long John. You see, he and the pirates got themselves engaged as the crew, and when we got to the island they mutinied, and now they've got the map showing where to find Flint's treasure. And the Squire and Dr. Livesey and Captain Smollett are prisoners on board the *Hispaniola*, but they've got guns hidden, and they'll probably escape before long. I want to hide from Silver until the Squire and the others can get ashore.

BEN: And then what'll you do, Jim, my lad?

JIM (*bravely*): Why, fight and kill the lot, find the treasure ourselves and sail the *Hispaniola* safe and sound home to Bristol.

BEN (*cackles*): Three men and a boy against Flint's old crew? Why, boy, they'd cut you down in half an hour.

The distant sound of shots is heard.

JIM: Listen! They've begun to fight. Oh, what shall we do, Mr. Gunn? What shall we do? We *must* help them.

BEN: Lookit, Jim. Is your Squire a gentleman?

JIM: Oh, yes, Mr. Gunn, I'm sure he is.

BEN: And would he, in return for a little help, be willing, say, to give a man a thousand pounds or two? Out of money, mark you, which is as good as his own already.

JIM: Oh, yes, I know he would.

BEN: *And* a passage home?

JIM: Oh, yes, besides, we should want you to help work the ship home. But, what can we do now to help the Squire?

BEN GUNN *produces a dagger.*

BEN: You'd be surprised what one man can do if he has a mind to it—and I know this island like the back of my hand. After all, I've been here for three years, matey, and I ain't been doing nothing. (*Cackles.*)

JIM: How did you come to be marooned, Mr. Gunn?

BEN: Well, I'll tell you, Jim. I were in Flint's ship when he buried the treasure. He went ashore with six men—six, big, husky pirates, mark you, Jim. He was ashore a week burying that treasure, and when the longboat came back, he was in it alone. White as a sheet he was, but all the six were dead—dead and buried. How he done it, not a man aboard could make out. It was battle, murder and sudden death. Him against six.

JIM: Golly!

BEN: Then I was in another ship three years back and we sighted this island. 'Boys,' says I, 'here's Flint's treasure. Let's land and find it.' 'Right,' says they, 'we will.' So they lowers a longboat and they comes ashore. Twelve days they looked for it and every day they got more and more displeased with me, until one fine morning they all went aboard. 'As for you, Ben Gunn,' says they, 'here's a spade and a pickaxe. You can stay and find Flint's treasure for yourself.' And off they goes, laughing. Well, I looked and I looked and now *I'm* laughing. (*Bursts into roars of hysterical laughter and dances about the stage clapping his hands. He stops suddenly and listens. Whispers.*) Listen, Jim.

JIM (*whispers*): What is it?

BEN: Quiet, ain't it? (*Briskly.*) Now, Jim. You creep down to the beach. Quietly, mind; and if there's no one about, set the longboats adrift—both of them, mind!

JIM: But, what will you do, Mr. Gunn?

BEN: I'll be a sort of one man reception committee for me old shipmates. (*Testing knife's edge.*) Who, unless my ears deceive me are coming this way now. Right, lad, off you go.

Exit JIM *left.* BEN GUNN *hides behind a tree right. There is a pause. Enter* LONG JOHN SILVER *followed by* TOM MORGAN, BLACK DOG *and* DEAD BONES JONES *right.*

SILVER: Damn and blast the green hide of that pickle-gutted blue-nosed Squire. Israel Hands and George Merry gone. As brave a pair as ever cut an honest throat! And now there's the three of them, armed, roaming the island. We'll have to be wary, Tom (*taps the side of his nose*) we'll have to be wary.

BLACK DOG: I think I may have wounded one of them as they came ashore. They were a fair distance away, but one of them staggered.

MORGAN: What I'd like to know is—where did they get them guns?

BLACK DOG: I'll stake my seaboots it was that blasted boy. I told you, Long John, we should have cut their throats aboard. You think you know more than the rest of us, just 'cos you been educated.

SILVER: And so I does, Black Dog. There's times when reading and writing does more than shot and shell. (*Sanctimoniously.*) The pen is mightier than the sword. (*A faint cry is heard.*) Did you hear something?

BLACK DOG: No.

SILVER: I thought I did.

MORGAN: We're wasting time, Long John. We've done enough bungling already. From now on we'll take majority decisions. (*Meaningly.*) Like we did when we tipped the Black Spot to Billy Bones.

SILVER: And would you be meaning by that, Mr. Morgan, that you were thinking of tipping me the Black Spot?

MORGAN: I ain't saying 'Yes' and I ain't saying 'No', but what I say is, 'There's work to be done; there's treasure to be found, and there's gizzards to be slit.' And talking won't do neither.

SILVER (*his back is to the others. It can be plainly seen by the expression on his face that he is scheming something*): Where are the others?

JONES: Dirk's keeping watch up ahead, and I left Johnny behind us as lookout.

SILVER: You two go and find Johnny, and you, Tom, Dirk, and bring them back. We'd best all stick together from now on.

MORGAN: Ar! I reckon you're right in that.

Exit BLACK DOG, TOM MORGAN *and* JONES. LONG JOHN *ruminates a moment and takes the centre of the stage.*

SILVER: I'm not sure as how I likes the way the wind is now a'blowing. And if the wind changes direction, Long John, then you'll have to change direction too. Aye, that you will. It'ld be a pretty pass indeed if the mutineer was mutinied upon himself. I don't trust Black Dog and I don't trust Tom Morgan. Come to think of it, I don't even trust Long John Silver. And I know how these pirates' minds work. To their way of thinking gold is worth more than Silver. Still, we'll wait and see.

Enter BLACK DOG *hurriedly.*

BLACK DOG: Long John! Long John!

SILVER: Well, did you find him.

BLACK DOG: Yes, but he's dead! His throat's been cut from ear to ear!

Enter TOM MORGAN *and* JONES *hurriedly left.*

JONES: He's been stabbed—Dirk—he's been stabbed!

SILVER: What!!

MORGAN: And more besides, Long John! I drew my cutlass and had a look round, and I saw something drop from a tree and run.

SILVER: What do you mean—some*thing*?

MORGAN: Well, I only caught a glimpse of it—but it looked half-way twixt man and beast.

BLACK DOG: Maybe the island is haunted. Let's get back to the ship.

MORGAN: We can't do that neither. I looked out to sea, and both the boats are adrift. Someone must have cut the ropes. That means we can't get back to get more powder and we've none left.

BLACK DOG (*drawing cutlass*): It's all your fault, Long John. You got us into this mess, and by thunder, you'll get us out or pay with your life!

SILVER (*scornfully*): Put up that cutlass, you fool. Three

can fight no better than four, and though I've only one leg I've still the beating in me of any of those landlubbers. So calm yourself, Dog, and let's get out of this before we're taken unawares.

The PIRATES *are now up stage left. They go off right with* JONES *in the rear. As* JONES *gets about half-way across the stage* BEN GUNN *swings on the stage on the end of a creeper and pounces on him, knife in hand. He kills him and drags him off stage. There is a pause. The* PIRATES *return.*

MORGAN: But he was right behind me, I tell you, and then I turned round to say something and he wasn't there.

SILVER: Well, he can't have vanished.

BLACK DOG: It doesn't matter what it was. We started with eight, and now we're three. Three against three, see? And that's not counting that blasted boy what you taught to use a cutlass. That's too damned even for me. I say let's get away while we can and hang the treasure. We've got the map, we can always come back again.

SILVER: Come back again? With what? Where would we get money enough for provisions—*and* a crew we could trust? No, Dog, here we are and here we stay, this is our only chance.

MORGAN: But what can we do? There's as many of them as us now. More, if you count Jim Hawkins.

SILVER: Listen, if we use our loafs, we'll outsmart 'em yet, and Ah ha—(*looking off left*) unless my old eyes deceive me, that's our old friend Master Hawkins approaching. (*Drawing cutlass and moving up stage of* JIM's *entrance.*) And I would have words with him.

The other PIRATES *join him, cutlasses drawn.* JIM *approaches whistling a sea-shanty.* MORGAN *and* BLACK DOG *behind and on either side of* SILVER *raise their cutlasses.* JIM'S *whistling gets louder as* . . .

CURTAIN

ACT III

Scene 1

The same as Act II Scene II.

Time. One second later.

Enter Jim *whistling.* Black Dog *leaps forward and seizes him raising his cutlass.*

Jim: Let me go! Let me go!

Silver: Stop that, you fool.

Jim: Let me go! I'm not afraid of you!

Black Dog: Stop it? Why? Now we've got the weevil let's have done with him before he does us any more harm.

Silver: Why? Because I say so.

Black Dog: And why should you always be having the say-so?

Silver (*drawing cutlass*): Avant there! Who are you, Black Dog? Maybe you think you're captain here. By the Powers, but I'll teach you better. Cross me, and you'll go where many a good man's gone before you these twenty years back—some by the yard-arm and some by the board—but all to feed the fishes. There's never a man that looked me between the eyes and saw a good day afterwards, Black Dog, you may lay to that. (Black Dog *lowers his cutlass grudgingly.*) Now, tell me, what have you got for brains? Barnacles? My very good friend, Jim Hawkins. . . .

JIM: I'm no friend of yours—not any more. You're a lot of bilge rats, that's what you are!

SILVER: Now then, Jim, you mustn't be rude to your elders. As I was saying, young Jim here, of whom let me say here and now I am very fond, is h'our ticket to Brist'hole.

MORGAN: How do you mean?

SILVER: Because with this lad as hostage, the Squire and his mates will be politely invited to dig up the treasure for us and help us sail the ship to Maracaibo, where we'll pick up a crew of trusty seamen and head for home. Two days out at sea we'll drop young Jim here and his pals off in a longboat, with a sail, and sufficient vittals to get them back to port. By the time they find a ship to follow us we shall be safe at home in Bristol, the treasure divided, and on our way to roam the four corners of the earth as gentlemen of leisure. (*Unseen by* JIM, *he winks at the others and makes a sign of cutting a throat.*)

MORGAN (*in an obviously insincere voice*): Why, h'I do believe that you h'are right, Long John, for h'after h'all, we wouldn't want to 'arm a hair on the 'ead of young Jim 'ere. Eh, Black Dog?

BLACK DOG (*in a similar voice*): Indeed you are right, Thomas. (*Winking.*) We will do as you suggest, Long John.

SILVER: That's better, lads. Now, let's scour the island to find them. If I'm righti n my calculations, we'll be on our way to Maracaibo by sundown.

They all go off, JIM *struggling and protesting. A pause. Enter* SQUIRE, DOCTOR *and* SMOLLETT, SQUIRE *wounded in right arm.*

SQUIRE: I can go no further for the moment, Livesey. I must rest. (*He sinks to the ground.*)

DR. LIVESEY: Things look pretty bad, Smollett. That rogue, Silver, has the map, and for all we know, he may have Jim, too. I'm afraid for the lad's life. They'll stop at nothing to get that treasure.

SMOLLETT: I'm afraid you're right. The powder that Jim got for us was just enough to get us off the ship. (*He holds up his pistol.*) I have not one shot left. But what's worse, is that we've only two cutlasses.

DR. LIVESEY: How badly are we outnumbered?

SMOLLETT: Six to two. Silver, Johnny, Dirk, Dead Bones, and that bearded cut-throat, Black Dog, against you and me. How badly is the Squire hit?

DR. LIVESEY: It's only a flesh wound, but he can't fight. What do you think we should do?

SMOLLETT: There's only one thing we can do, Doctor. Stay here until we find Jim. Hide until darkness, when I shall swim out to the *Hispaniola* and bring back a longboat. I'll pick you up, return to the ship, collect provisions, and try to sail to Maracaibo.

SQUIRE: How far is Maracaibo?

SMOLLETT: About a hundred miles, but the weather looks set for a few days. We should get there without much trouble.

SQUIRE: What if Silver has got Jim?

DR. LIVESEY: In that case there is only one thing for it— a fight to the death! Agreed?

SQUIRE AND SMOLLETT: Agreed

DR. LIVESEY: We can't hope to win, but we shall sell our lives dearly.

SMOLLETT: I'd like to get a cut at Silver.

DR. LIVESEY: Strangely enough, I can't help liking Silver in spite of the fact that he's an out-and-out rogue. It's that Black Dog whose claret I'd like to tap. (*Making an imaginary swipe with his cutlass.*)

VOICE OFF: Flag o' truce! Flag o' truce!

SQUIRE (*struggling to his feet*): Who is it, Livesey?

DR. LIVESEY: It's Silver. He's waving a white flag. What do you think it means, Smollett?

SMOLLETT: I don't know, but we had best talk to him. Maybe we can find out if they've got Jim.

DR. LIVESEY: I agree with you. Ahoy, there, Silver. Come forward.

Enter SILVER *carrying a white flag.* BEN GUNN *appears, and darts out of sight.*

SILVER: Good-day to ye, gentlemen. Captain Silver, come aboard to have words with you. (*He bows.*)

SMOLLETT: Captain Silver, indeed! Long John Silver, my ship's cook turned mutineer and pirate!

SILVER: Ah, Captain. Them's harsh words. Who can blame a poor retired buccaneer for trying to get a little nest-egg for his old age?

DR. LIVESEY: Enough of this nonsense, Silver. Say what you have to say and begone!

SQUIRE: Aye, before I lose patience and forget that flag of truce.

SILVER (*with a grin*): Don't forget that, Squire. I had

terrible trouble to persuade Tom Morgan to let me have it. (*He displays his flag of truce, which is a pair of long underpants with innumerable holes in them.*) What I came to tell you was this—I have the map of the treasure.

DR. LIVESEY: We know that, Silver, we gave it to you.

SILVER: Indeed you did, Doctor. But I also have something else you didn't give me, something I sort of found, like, and it goes by the name of Hawkins.

SQUIRE: You swine!

SILVER: Now, you've no call to be abusive, Squire, for I'm only doing my best by me shipmates. Now I've no wish to be sniped at while I'm digging for the treasure, nor while I'm building a raft to take me back to the ship. Nor do I fancy sailing the *Hispaniola* with a crew of three. So me proposition is this—Leave us free to find the treasure. Help us to sail the ship to Maracaibo. Once in Maracaibo, I'll hire me a crew and set sail for home. Two days out of port I'll set you off in a longboat with a sail and vittals, so as you can get back to port and wait for a ship to England. What do you say to that? Them couldn't be fairer terms if you made them up yourselves.

DR. LIVESEY: That's all very well, Silver, but how do we know you're not bluffing? We've only got your word to take that you've got Jim, and you know how much your word's worth.

SILVER: You're on the right tack there, Doctor, so how about me slipping off and cutting off an ear to show you?

SQUIRE: No! No!

SILVER: It's quite all right. No trouble, I assure you. Or maybe you'd prefer a finger?

SMOLLETT: Wait a minute, while we talk it over. (*They move aside.*)

SQUIRE: So they've got Jim.

DR. LIVESEY: Yes, things look pretty black.

SMOLLETT: Silver said a crew of three. What can have happened to the other three?

DR. LIVESEY: Perhaps they fell out and fought.

SMOLLETT: At any rate, what do you think about his offer? Can we trust him?

DR. LIVESEY: I'm afraid we'll have to. If we try and fight them, they'll kill Jim, and we'll probably be killed ourselves. If we agree to his terms, at least we save Jim temporarily. Silver may keep his word—there's always a chance of that. And if he looks like going back on it later, we still have a chance of fighting then. What do you say, Squire?

SQUIRE: Is there no other way out?

DR. LIVESEY: None that I can see.

SQUIRE: In that case, I agree.

DR. LIVESEY: You, Smollett? (SMOLLETT *nods and they turn towards* SILVER.) Very well, Silver. We agree to your offer. We'll retire to the other side of the island and leave you to find the treasure in peace. And we give you our word not to harm you. We'll meet you at this spot at the same time tomorrow. Agreed?

SILVER: Agreed, Doctor. I think you're behaving most sensible. (*Sincerely.*) It would have grieved me more than I can say to harm that lad, for to tell you the truth, I've grown quite fond of him. 'Ah demang, Monsewers', as the Frenchies say. (*Exit* SILVER *left.*)

SQUIRE: You know, I think he meant that.

DR. LIVESEY: I hope so. It'd be a pity if all Jim's bravery were to come to naught.

SMOLLETT: Do you think they'll find the treasure by tomorrow?

DR. LIVESEY: I should think so. The map was pretty clear.

SQUIRE: When I think of what an ass I've been I could kick myself.

DR. LIVESEY: Oh, it's not your fault, Squire. Almost anyone would have been taken in by that smooth-tongued rascal.

SMOLLETT: Yes, it looks like he's beaten us.

SQUIRE: Do you think we shall ever see England again?

DR. LIVESEY: That, my dear Squire, only time will tell.

SQUIRE: Well, in that case, gentlemen, there's nothing we can do but wait.

They all go off left. A pause. BEN GUNN *darts on. He looks off right and giggles. He looks off left and giggles. He returns to the centre of the stage and rolls on his back in a fit of uncontrollable laughter, kicking his legs in the air, crying . . .* Pieces of eight! Pieces of eight!

CURTAIN

Scene 2

The same.
Time. The next day.
Enter Long John Silver.

Silver: The wind's changed all right. It's blowing half a gale. You'll be lucky to get out of this, Long John, my boy, with your life, let alone any treasure. You're not the man you used to be. What you could have done twenty years ago to that swab Morgan, you can't do today. Oh! Where could it have gone? Nothing but empty chests! Who could have known? Flint killed the six that went ashore with him and he only made one map. Still, it's no use crying over spilt milk. The thing is now, what to do? Here's Black Dog and Morgan on the one hand, ready to stick a knife in me at the drop of a hat. Oh! I never saw two more disgruntled gentlemen of fortune in all my life! And the Squire and the Captain on the other hand, with nothing to offer but a hangman's noose. No, which ever way it goes, you're for fire and brimstone, Master Silver! Still, it's been a good life. When I think of the good tall ships I've sailed in, and the wine and the wenches, I've nary a regret. But I'll not live like a lion and die like a lamb. Oh, no! That's not John Silver's way. I'll see if I can't right a little of the wrong I've done Jim Hawkins. He's a fine lad to be sure, and maybe if I'd had a son . . . but, ah! well! what's the use of talking . . . doing's the word!

Enter right Tom Morgan *and* Black Dog, *with a still defiant* Jim Hawkins.

BLACK DOG (*growls*): Any sign of 'em?

SILVER (*jovially*): None yet, mateys, but never fear, they gave their word, and they're gentlemen born and bred.

MORGAN (*spits*): Bah!

BLACK DOG: Keep an eye on Hawkins.

He pushes JIM *towards* LONG JOHN. LONG JOHN *and* JIM *are down right.* MORGAN *and* BLACK DOG *centre. During the ensuing conversation they talk in undertones, casting frequent glances at* SILVER.

SILVER (*out of the corner of his mouth in a stage whisper*): Jim!

JIM: Yes?

SILVER: Things is looking pretty black for us, matey.

JIM: What do you mean?

SILVER: I means that if I know my onions, and them two is as ugly a pair of onions as you'll ever see—the night before we reach Maracaibo, there'll be some slitting of throats, and yours and mine will be the first to go.

JIM: Gosh! (*Putting hand to throat.*)

SILVER: Now then, for no particular reason, other than I likes you, and wants to do some good before I dies, I'm going to help you out of this. Now, listen carefully. The Squire's got powder and shot, but we haven't, but the Squire don't know that. After your friends arrive, at a good moment, I'll let you go, and take a swipe at one of the others with my crutch. And from then on, Jim, boy, it's a fight.

JIM: But will you be all right?

SILVER: I don't know, lad. That doesn't matter. But you will, and that does matter.

JIM: That's awfully kind of you, Mr. Silver. And I'm sorry I called you a bilge rat.

SILVER: That's all right, matey. Now I come to think of it, I am a bilge rat.

SILVER *and* JIM *move up stage waiting for the* SQUIRE. BLACK DOG *and* TOM MORGAN *move down stage.*

BLACK DOG: I tell you, Tom, I'm sure of it. First chance he gets he'll cut our throats and have the treasure for himself.

MORGAN: But what are we to do about it? We can't sail the ship without him. That blasted sea captain would have us in irons before you could say knife.

BLACK DOG: We won't do nothing about it now, but later we'll do plenty.

MORGAN: Such as, what?

BLACK DOG: Such as, this. The night before we get to Maracaido you and I will do a little visiting with these. (*He produces a knife or indicates his cutlass.*)

MORGAN: I sees what you mean, Black Dog. Here's me hand on it. (*They both spit on their hands and shake.*)

VOICE OFF: Ahoy, there.

BLACK DOG *grabs* JIM *and he and* MORGAN *draw cutlasses. Enter the* SQUIRE, DR. LIVESEY *and* CAPTAIN SMOLLETT.

BLACK DOG: Good-day—*gentlemen.*

SMOLLETT: Good-day.

BLACK DOG: Well, where is it?

DR. LIVESEY: Where's what?

MORGAN: The treasure.

Squire: Why, haven't you got it?

Silver: No, sir, we haven't. And the boys are thinking that maybe you'd made a copy of the map and got there first.

Squire: We did no such thing. We gave you our word.

Black Dog: Word be damned! We found the spot, and we dug, and all there was was empty chests. The treasure's gone somewhere and we want to know where.

Smollett: I assure you, we know nothing of the treasure.

Black Dog: Oh yes? Then tell me, where *is* it?

Morgan: Aye! Where's it gone? Can't have vanished into thin air. Someone must have took it.

Smollett: We have absolutely no idea. We gave you the only map, and we spent the last twenty-four hours on the other side of the island.

Black Dog: All right then, I'll tell you what I'll do. I'll count ten, and on the stroke of ten . .

Smollett: You wouldn't.

Black Dog: That's where you're making a mistake, Captain. I would. On the stroke of ten, if you haven't come clean, I'll slit Jim Hawkins's throat.

Dr. Livesey: But I tell you . .

Black Dog: One!

Dr. Livesey: We know nothing of the treasure.

Black Dog: Two!

Squire: Not a thing, I assure you.

Black Dog: Three!

Smollett: Look here, Dog . . .

BLACK DOG: Four!

SMOLLETT: What you're doing . . .

BLACK DOG: Five!

SMOLLETT: Is cold blooded murder!

BLACK DOG: Six!

DR. LIVESEY: Is there nothing we can do!

BLACK DOG: Seven!

SQUIRE: We implore you . . .

BLACK DOG: Eight!

SQUIRE: Spare the boy!

BLACK DOG: Nine!

DR. LIVESEY: No! No!

As BLACK DOG *opens his mouth to say 'Ten'* LONG JOHN, *who has been standing close to him, hits him hard across the body with his crutch.* BLACK DOG *staggers backwards as* JIM *eludes his grasp and dashes across to his companions. The force of his blow has put* LONG JOHN *off balance and both he and* BLACK DOG *regain balance at the same time. As* LIVESEY *and* SMOLLETT *more forward, cutlasses in hand,* BLACK DOG *catches* LONG JOHN *a fierce blow with his cutlass.* LONG JOHN *staggers back wounded as the four men clash.* SMOLLETT *drives* TOM MORGAN *down stage left where he kills him, and at the same time* BLACK DOG *drives* LIVESEY *right, near to where* LONG JOHN *is standing.* BLACK DOG *knocks* LIVESEY'S *cutlass out of his hand and is about to strike when* LONG JOHN'S *intervention (either by crutch, cudgel or missile) gives* LIVESEY *the necessary second's respite for* SMOLLETT *to reach him and engage* BLACK DOG, *whom he quickly overcomes.*

SQUIRE: Well done, Smollett!

SMOLLETT: Look down there, Doctor, and make sure there are no more of these villains lurking around. You, Squire, that way. Are you all right, Jim?

JIM: Yes, thank you. They didn't hurt me at all.

SMOLLETT: Well, any signs, Squire?

SQUIRE: No.

DR. LIVESEY: Not a trace.

SMOLLETT: Well, I never thought to see those rascals dead, and this villain (*pointing to* LONG JOHN SILVER) in our power.

JIM: Oh, but he's not a villain.

DR. LIVESEY: Indeed, no. He saved my life.

SQUIRE: I can't understand the fellow. Perhaps he's drunk.

JIM: No, he's not drunk. When the others had me, he told me he was going to help me to escape. He knew he was risking his life, but he did it because he felt sorry for what he had done. You mustn't harm him.

SMOLLETT: That's all very well, but you know as well as I do what this man is. He's lied, stolen, and murdered his way through life. He's the worst sort of sea scum. It would be a crime to let him escape. We mustn't soften just because he helped Jim. If things had gone his way, he would have been the first to suggest cutting our throats, wouldn't you?

LONG JOHN *is standing with his hand across his chest.*

SILVER: I'll not lie to you, Captain. If we had found the treasure you would've all been fed to the sharks.

SMOLLETT: There—you see?

SQUIRE: I don't care what you say, Smollett, by his action he saved our lives, and to harm him now would be most un-English.

JIM: Oh, please, please let him go. Can't you see he's hurt?

The DOCTOR *moves quickly over to* LONG JOHN *as he staggers.*

SILVER: No matter, Doctor. It's only a scratch.

DR. LIVESEY: Well, let me bind it for you.

The DOCTOR, *using his own and* SILVER's *handkerchief, binds his wounded arm.*

SQUIRE: What I can't understand is what happened to the treasure. Couldn't you find the spot, Silver?

SILVER: We found the spot all right, Squire, but someone had been there before us.

SMOLLETT: Could it have been the others? Dirk, Johnny and Dead Bones?

SILVER: No, it couldn't have been them, Captain. Dirk and Johnny is dead, and Dead Bones is disappeared.

SQUIRE: What? How did that happen?

SILVER: Didn't you kill them?

SQUIRE: Me?

DR. LIVESEY: We haven't seen anyone on the island except these two and you. What exactly happened?

SILVER: We left Dirk and Johnny as lookouts, and when we went to fetch them they'd been killed. We thought it was you. And then we went down the hill, and Dead Bones just disappeared!

SMOLLETT: I can't understand it. We've not seen him, and we certainly didn't kill the others.

JIM: Wait a minute. I think I know who killed them.

SMOLLETT: Who?

JIM: A man called . . .

VOICE OFF: Ben Gunn.

SQUIRE: What was that?

JIM: I think that was . . .

BEN GUNN (*entering with a flourish*): Ben Gunn!

The others stare at him.

DR. LIVESEY: What, in the name of all that's holy, is *that*?

SILVER: Well, if it isn't my old shipmate, Ben Gunn.

BEN: *Hallo*, Long John. You're keeping mighty fine company. Not like the old days, eh? Your 'umble servant, sirs. You don't happen to 'ave a piece of cheese on you, do you?

SMOLLETT: Of course not.

BEN: Are you sure? I've a mortal longing for a piece of cheese.

SQUIRE: Well, it so happens I have brought a little ashore, in case of emergencies, you know . . .

He tails off, embarrassed, and produces a small piece of cheese from his pocket which BEN GUNN *seizes and gobbles with obvious delight.*

SMOLLETT: Who is this man? And what is he doing on the island?

JIM: He's been marooned here for three years. He landed to look for Captain Flint's treasure and he's been here ever since. It was he who told me to cut the longboats adrift, and he offered to help us. I promised that if he did we would give him a free passage home, and two thousand guineas.

SQUIRE: Two thousand guineas? After what this trip's cost me, I haven't even two hundred guineas. It's absolutely out of the question.

BEN: Ah! But what you don't know is—I've got something that you would like.

DR. LIVESEY: You don't mean . . .

SMOLLETT: You weren't the one . . .

SQUIRE: I don't believe it!

BEN: Cap-ee-tin Fer-lint's ter-easure.

SILVER: You mean, *you* dug it up?

BEN (*clapping his hands and skipping*): Yes, yes!

JIM: Was there lots of it?

BEN: Lots? Why, Master Hawkins, enough to ransom fifty kings, *and* buy your lady friend a new bonnet!

JIM: Were there any doubloons?

BEN: Doubloons!

JIM: Guineas?

BEN: Guineas!

JIM: Pieces of eight?

BEN: Pieces of eight? Pieces of eight?? Thowwsands (*rushing round clapping his hands*) and thowwsands and *thowwsands!!*

JIM: Where is it, Mr. Gunn?

BEN: If I get these gentlemen's promise, a passage home

and two thousand guineas, I'll take you there. *And cheese.* Slices and slices of cheese.

SQUIRE: You have my word on it. All the cheese in the world. Well, Jim, this is a happy ending, and it's all thanks to you. I never expected our voyage to end like this. Not after what happened yesterday.

This focuses attention of all on LONG JOHN SILVER.

DR. LIVESEY: The question is, what shall we do with Long John?

JIM: I say, let him go.

DR. LIVESEY: And so do I.

SQUIRE (*heartily*): And so do I.

SMOLLETT: Will you help us work the ship home, Silver?

SILVER: Aye, gladly, Captain.

SMOLLETT: Then I will agree with the others.

JIM: Hooray! Hooray! (*Going to* LONG JOHN.)

SMOLLETT: Well, we had best be off to collect the treasure, and then back to the ship. If we hurry we'll be away before sundown.

BEN (*leaping in the air*): Hey-ho! Hey-ho! to work we go.

He starts to go off. LIVESEY, *the* SQUIRE *and* SMOLLETT *follow him with* LONG JOHN *bringing up the rear holding* JIM's *hand. Before anyone can get off stage* LONG JOHN SILVER *starts to sing.*

SILVER: Fifteen men on a ..
    (JIM *joins in*)
    dead man's chest.

As JIM *and* LONG JOHN *sing the next line*—Yo-ho-ho and

a bottle of rum—*the others turn and look at them, break into smiles and join in as they go off.*

ALL: Drink and the devil had done for the rest—
Yo-ho-ho and a bottle of rum!

CURTAIN